EASY PIANO

2013 GREATEST CHRISTIAN Hits

Arranged by Carol Tornquist

Produced by
Alfred Music
P.O. Box 10003
Van Nuys, CA 91410-0003
alfred.com

Printed in USA.

ISBN-10: 0-7390-9613-3
ISBN-13: 978-0-7390-9613-0

Cover Photo
Concert Crowd: © istockphoto / miappv

D0907695

Alfred Cares. Contents printed on 100% recycled paper.

CONTENTS

Song	Artist	Page
10,000 Reasons (Bless the Lord)	Matt Redman	3
God's Not Dead (Like a Lion)	Newsboys	6
Good Morning	Mandisa	11
Hold Me	Jamie Grace featuring TobyMac	14
How Great Is Our God	Chris Tomlin	18
I Need a Miracle	Third Day	22
Jesus, Friend of Sinners	Casting Crowns	25
Need You Now (How Many Times)	Plumb	30
One Thing Remains	Passion featuring Kristian Stanfill	35
The Proof of Your Love	For King & Country	40
Redeemed	Big Daddy Weave	44
We Are	Kari Jobe	48
Who You Are	Unspoken	52
Whom Shall I Fear (God of Angel Armies)	Chris Tomlin	55
You Are	Colton Dixon	58
Your Love Never Fails	Newsboys	61

10,000 REASONS (BLESS THE LORD)

Words and Music by
Matt Redman and Jonas Myrin
Arranged by Carol Tornquist

4

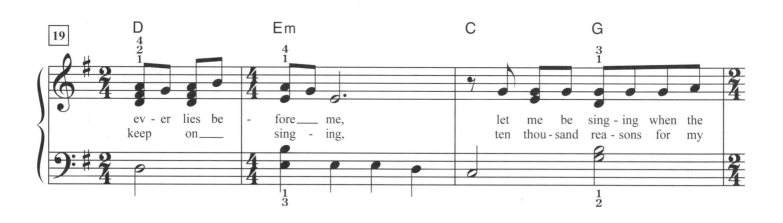

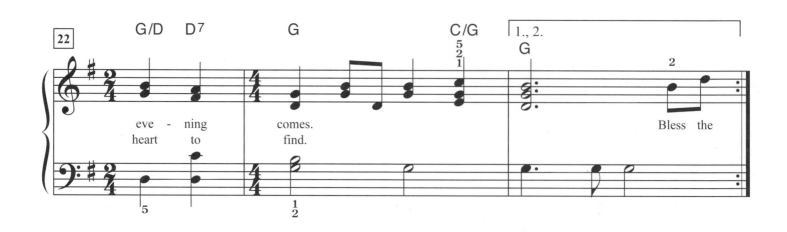

Verse 3:
And on that day when my strength is failing,
The end draws near and my time has come;
Still, my soul will sing Your praise unending,
Ten thousand years and then forevermore.
(To Chorus:)

GOD'S NOT DEAD (LIKE A LION)

Words and Music by Daniel Bashta
Arranged by Carol Tornquist

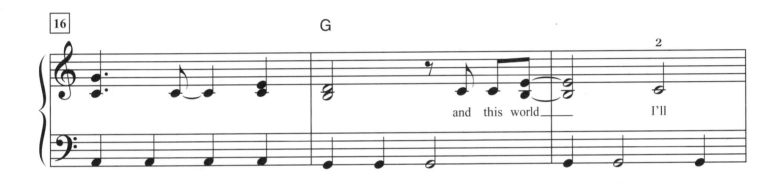

Chorus:

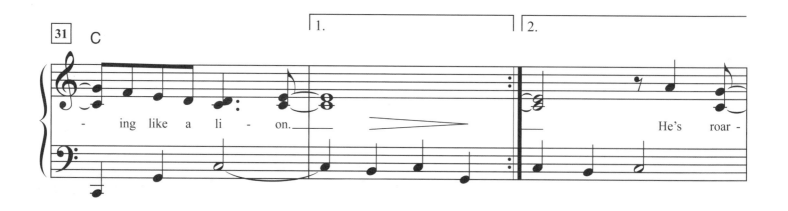

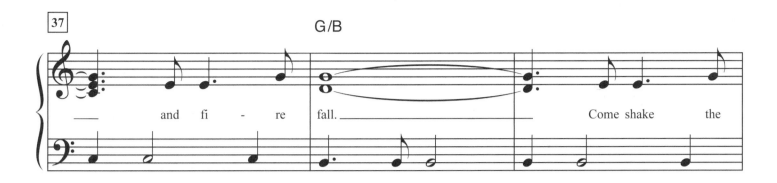

and fi - re fall. Come shake the

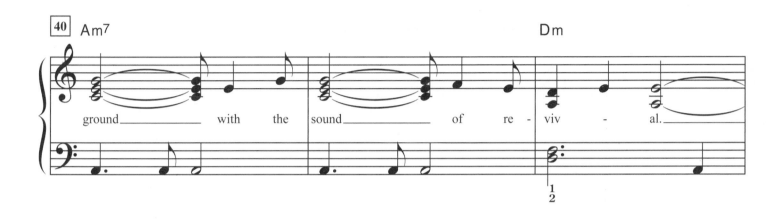

ground with the sound of re - viv - al.

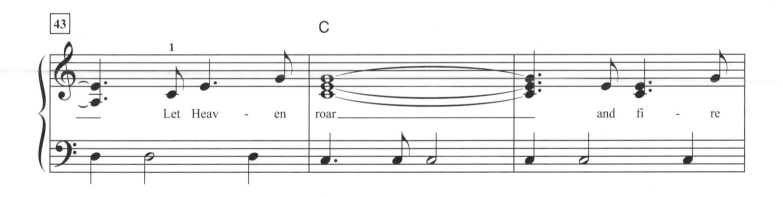

Let Heav - en roar and fi - re

fall. Come shake the ground with the

GOOD MORNING

Words and Music by Aaron Rice,
Cary Barlowe, Jamie Moore,
Mandisa Hundley and Toby McKeehan
Arranged by Carol Tornquist

Verse 2:
Slow down, breathe in, don't move ahead.
I'm just living in the moment.
I've got my arms raised, unphased, jump out of bed.
Gotta get this party going.
I went to bed dreaming.
You woke me up singing, "Get up, get up, hey!"
(To Chorus:)

HOLD ME

Words and Music by Chris Stevens,
Jamie Grace and Toby McKeehan
Arranged by Carol Tornquist

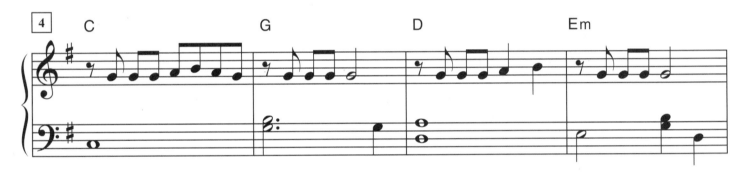

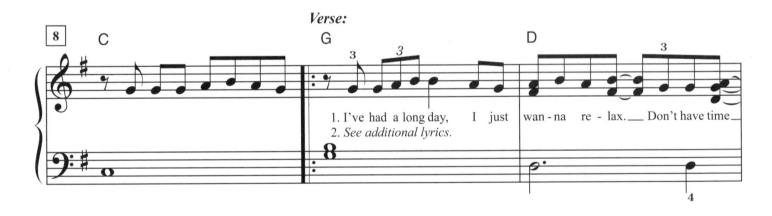

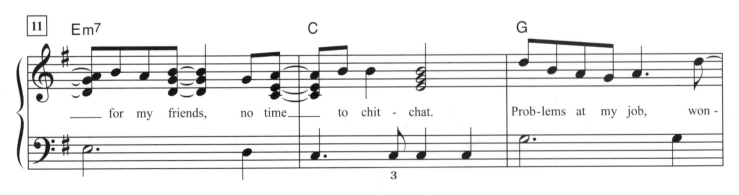

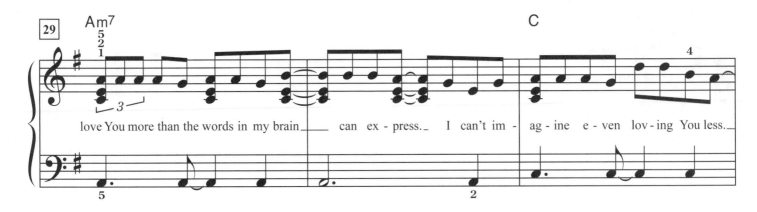

love You more than the words in my brain ___ can ex - press. ___ I can't im - ag - ine e - ven lov - ing You less.

___ Lord, I love the way You hold me. ___ Whoa, ___ oh, oh, ___ oh,

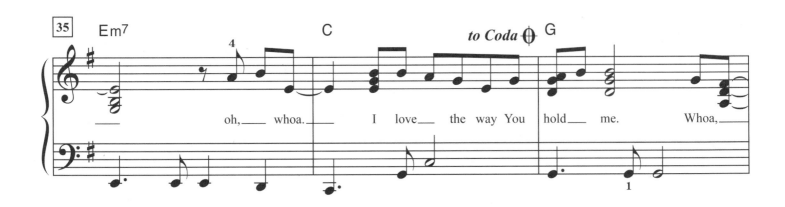

oh, ___ whoa. I love ___ the way You hold ___ me. Whoa,

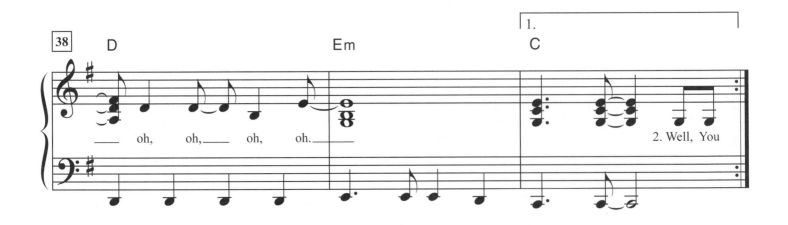

___ oh, oh, ___ oh, oh. ___ 2. Well, You

Verse 2:
Well, You took my day and You flipped it around,
Calmed the tidal wave and put my feet on the ground.
Forever in my heart, always on my mind,
It's crazy how I think about you all of the time.
And just when I think I'm 'bout to figure You out,
You make me wanna sing and shout.
(To Chorus:)

HOW GREAT IS OUR GOD

Words and Music by Jesse Reeves,
Chris Tomlin and Ed Cash
Arranged by Carol Tornquist

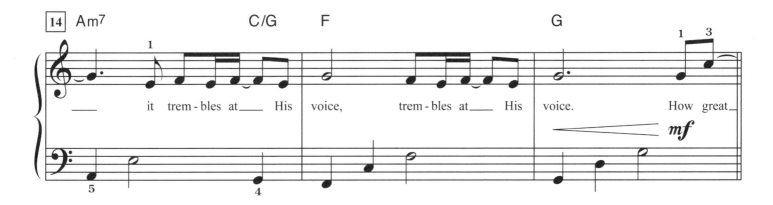

Chorus:

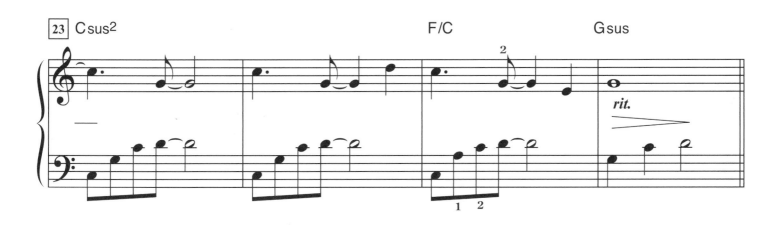

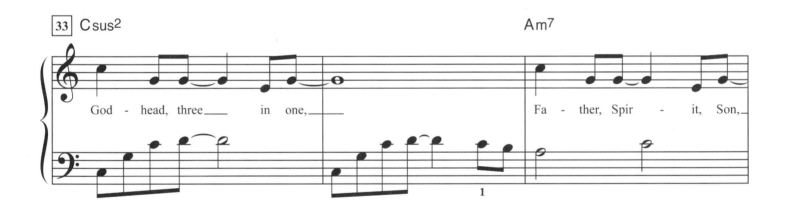

Chorus:

_____ is our God! ____ Sing with me, ____ "How great ____ is our God!"

____ And all will see how great, how great ____ is our God!

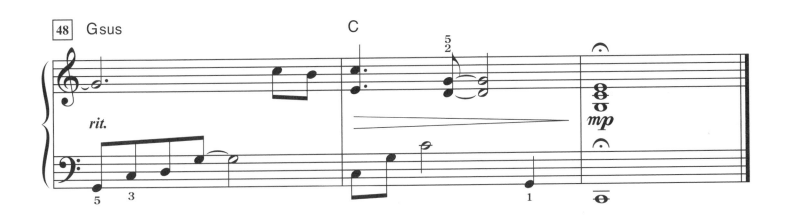

rit.

_mp_

I NEED A MIRACLE

Words and Music by David Carr,
Mac Powell, Mark Lee and Tai Anderson
Arranged by Carol Tornquist

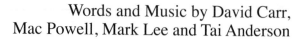

Verse 2:
He lost his job and all he had in the fall of '09.
Now he feared the worst, that he would lose his children and his wife.
So he drove down deep into the woods and thought he'd end it all,
And prayed, "Lord above, I need a miracle."
(To Chorus:)

Verse 3:
He turned on the radio to hear a song for the last time.
He didn't know what he was looking for or even what he'd find.
And the song he heard, it gave him hope and strength to carry on.
And on that night they found a miracle.
(To Chorus:)

JESUS, FRIEND OF SINNERS

Words and Music by
Matthew West and Mark Hall
Arranged by Carol Tornquist

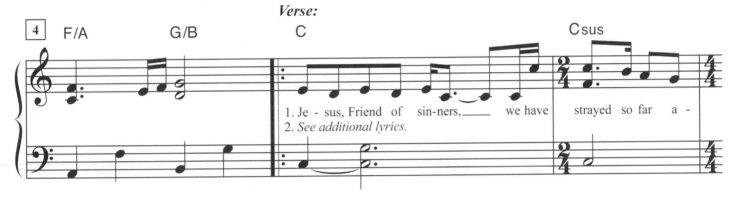

26

28

Verse 2:
Jesus, Friend of sinners, the One whose writing in the sand
Made the righteous turn away and the stones fall from their hands,
Help us to remember we are all the least of these.
Let the memory of Your mercy bring Your people to their knees.
Nobody knows what we're for, only what we're against when we judge the wounded.
What if we put down our signs, crossed over the lines and loved like You did?
(To Chorus:)

NEED YOU NOW (HOW MANY TIMES)

Words and Music by Christa Wells,
Luke Sheets and Tiffany Arbuckle
Arranged by Carol Tornquist

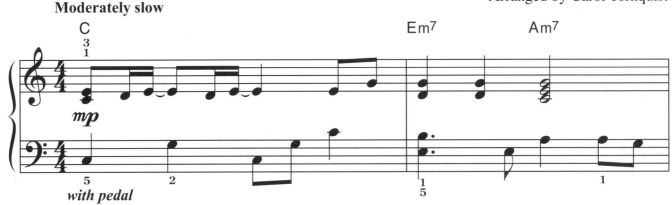

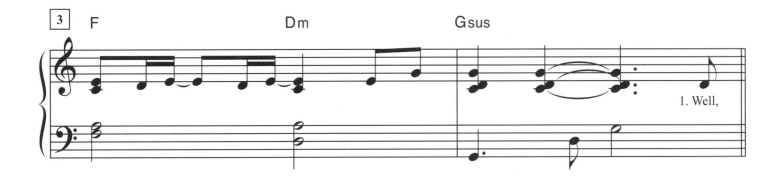

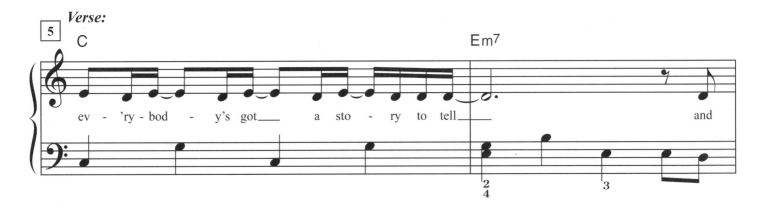

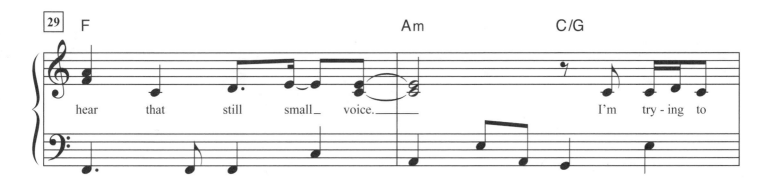

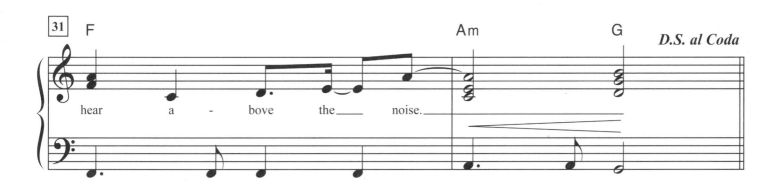

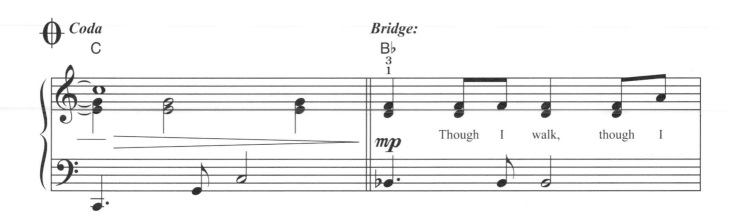

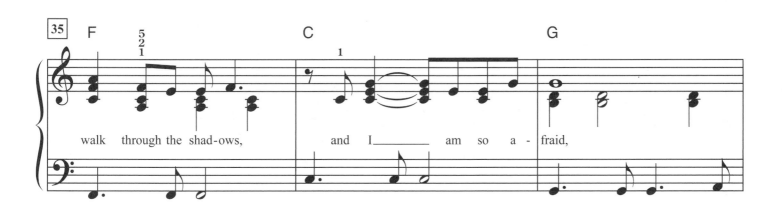

ONE THING REMAINS
(YOUR LOVE NEVER FAILS)

Words and Music by Jeremy Riddle,
Brian Johnson and Christa Black
Arranged by Carol Tornquist

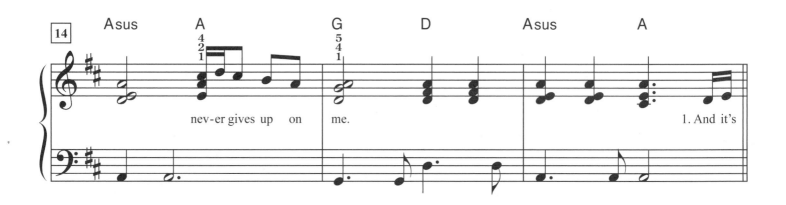

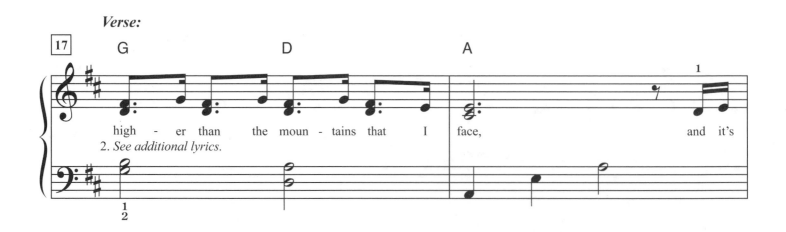

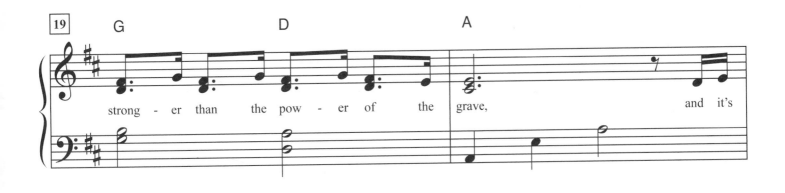

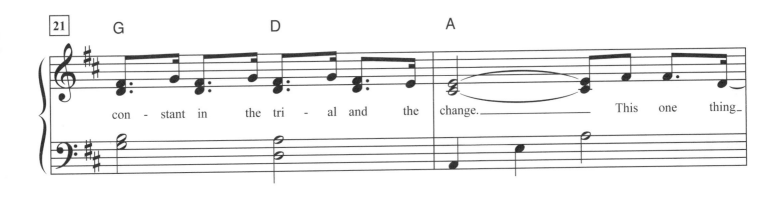

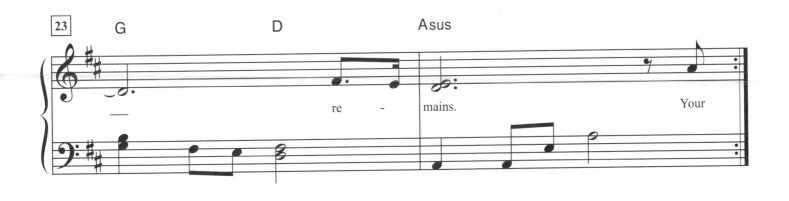

38

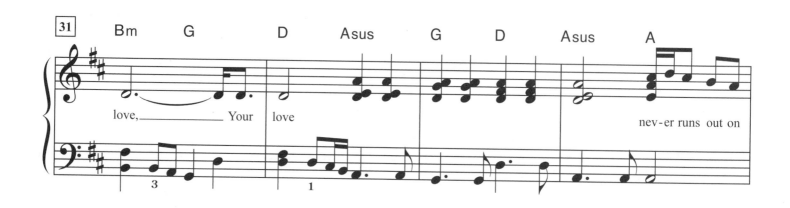

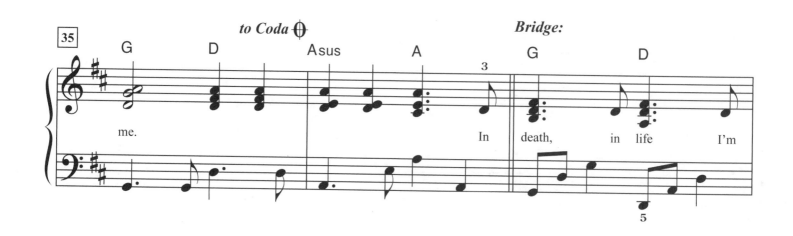

Verse 2:
And on and on and on and on it goes.
Yes, it overwhelms and satisfies my soul.
And I'll never, ever have to be afraid.
This one thing remains.
(To Chorus:)

THE PROOF OF YOUR LOVE

Words and Music by Luke Smallbone,
Joel David Smallbone, Ben Glover,
Frederick Williams, Jonathan Lee, and Mia Fieldes
Arranged by Carol Tornquist

Verse:

26 | B♭ — Dm — Am7 — B♭

give to a need-y soul but don't have love, then who is poor? It

28 | Gm7 — Dm — Am7 — B♭

seems all the pov-er - ty is found in me. So

Chorus:

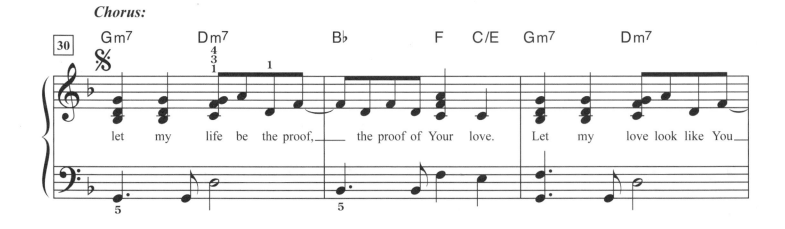

30 | Gm7 — Dm7 — B♭ — F — C/E — Gm7 — Dm7

let my life be the proof, the proof of Your love. Let my love look like You

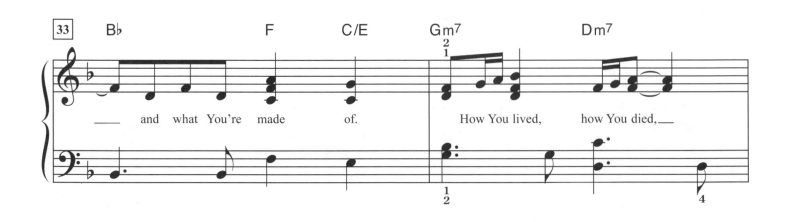

33 | B♭ — F — C/E — Gm7 — Dm7

and what You're made of. How You lived, how You died,

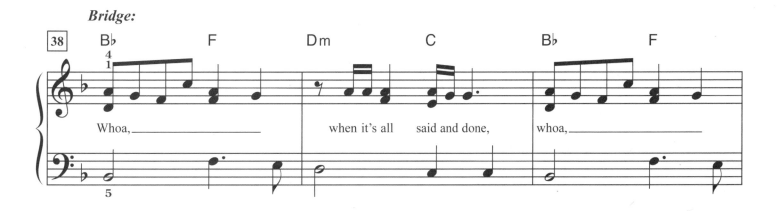

REDEEMED

Words and Music by
Benji Cowart and Michael Weaver
Arranged by Carol Tornquist

WE ARE

Words and Music by Ed Cash,
Chuck Butler, James Tealy and Hillary McBride
Arranged by Carol Tornquist

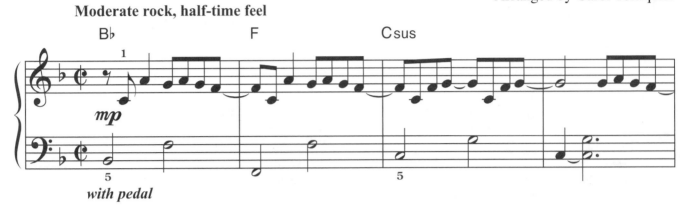

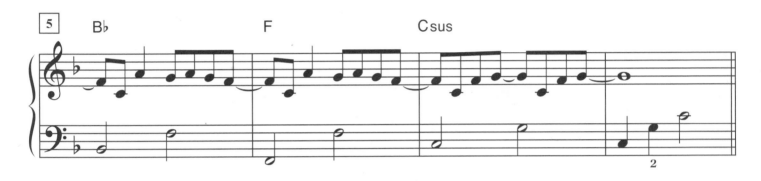

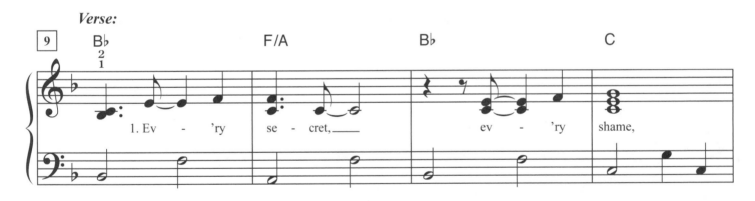

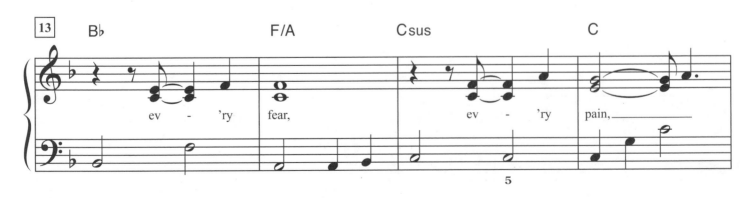

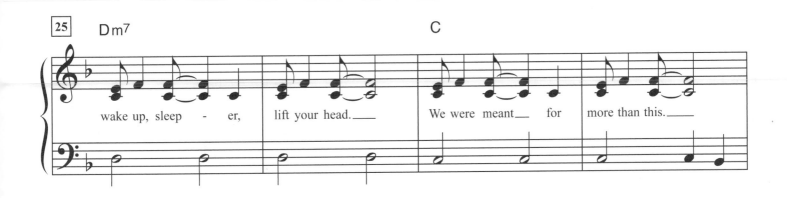

Chorus:

WHO YOU ARE

Words and Music by Jason Walker,
Michael Gomez, Chad Mattson and Jon Lowry
Arranged by Carol Tornquist

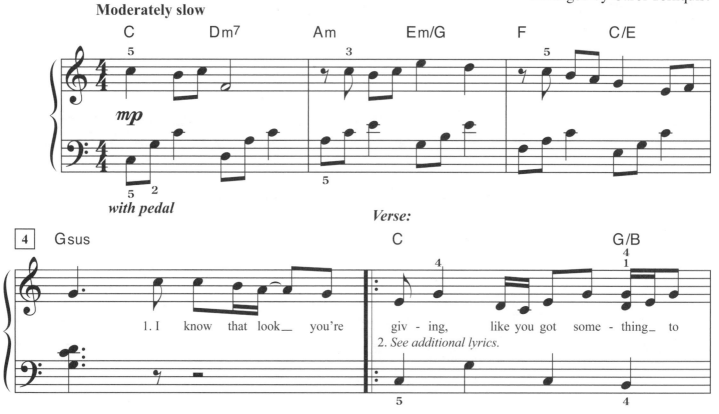

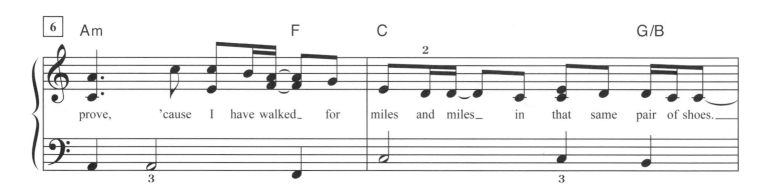

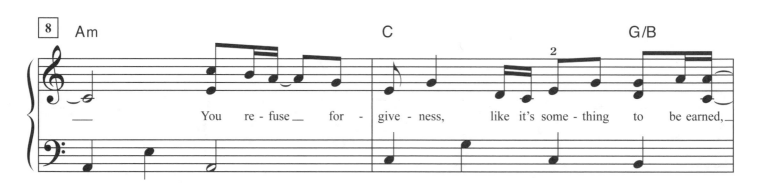

54

Bridge:

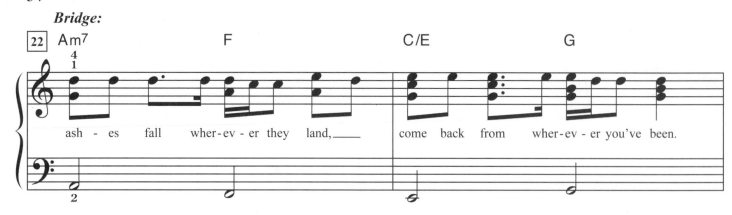

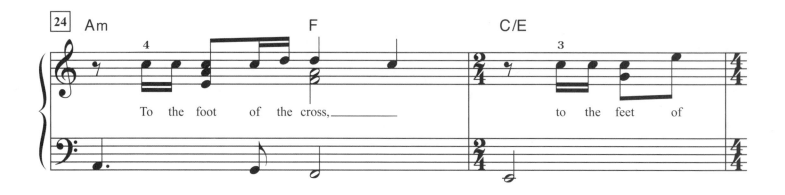

D.S. al Coda

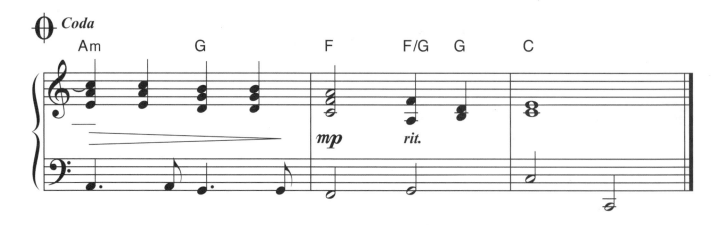

Verse 2:
You believe in freedom, but you don't know how to choose.
You gotta step out of your feelings that you're so afraid to lose.
And ev'ry day you put your feet on the floor, you gotta walk through the door.
It's never gonna be easy, but it's all worth fighting for.
(To Chorus:)

WHOM SHALL I FEAR
(GOD OF ANGEL ARMIES)

Words and Music by Chris Tomlin,
Ed Cash and Scott Cash
Arranged by Carol Tornquist

Chorus:

I know who goes be-fore me,__ I know who stands be-hind. The God of an-gel ar-mies

is al-ways by my side. The One who reigns for-ev-er,__ He is a friend of mine.

The God of an-gel ar-mies is al-ways by my side. And

Bridge:

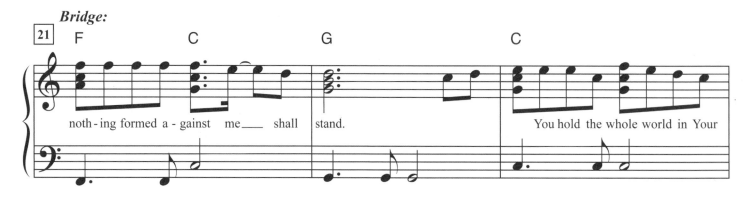

noth-ing formed a-gainst me__ shall stand. You hold the whole world in Your

hands. I'm hold-ing on to Your prom-is-es.__ You are

YOU ARE

Words and Music by Rhyan Shirley,
Jared Martin, Colton Dixon and Mike Busbee
Arranged by Carol Tornquist

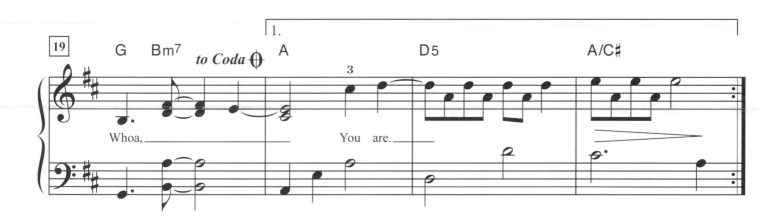

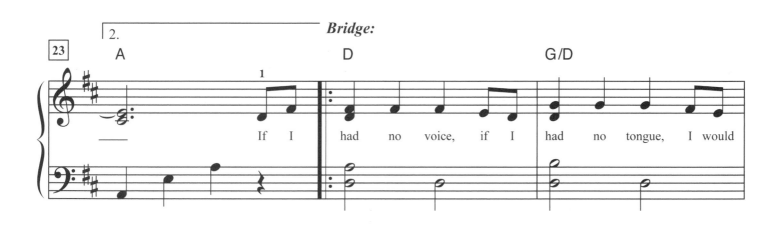

60

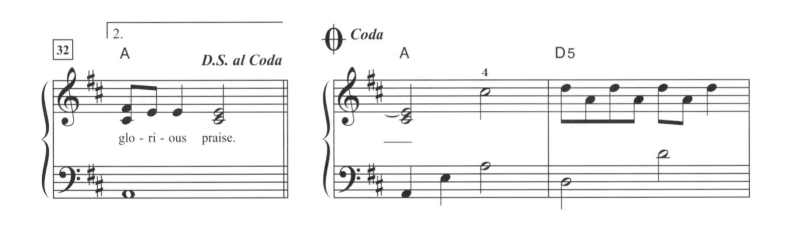

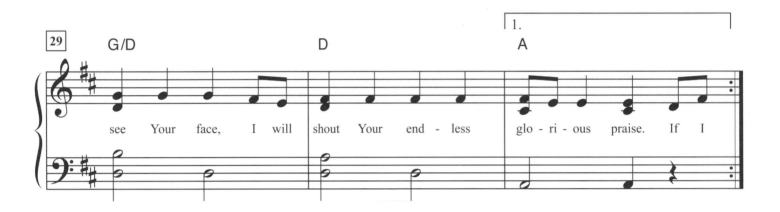

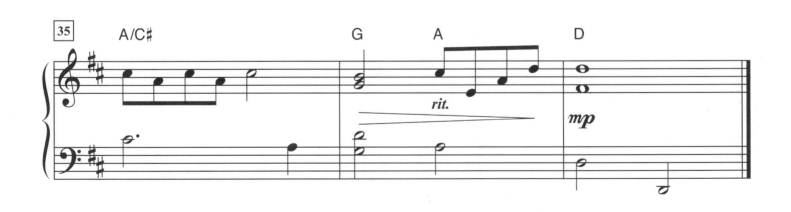

YOUR LOVE NEVER FAILS

Words and Music by
Anthony Skinner and Chris McClarney
Arranged by Carol Tornquist

Moderately, with a steady beat

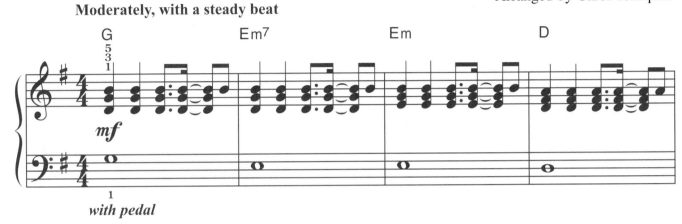

with pedal

Verse:

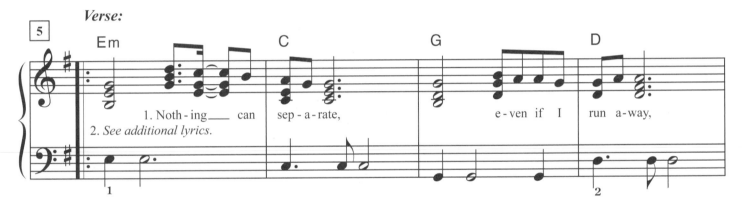

1. Noth-ing____ can sep-a-rate, e-ven if I run a-way,
2. *See additional lyrics.*

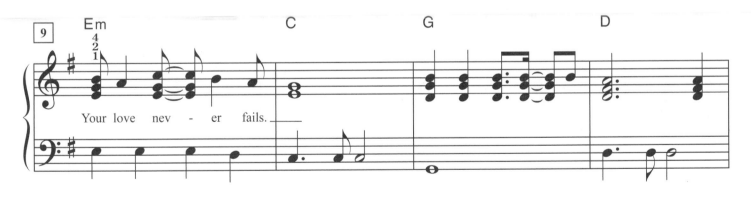

Your love nev - er fails.____

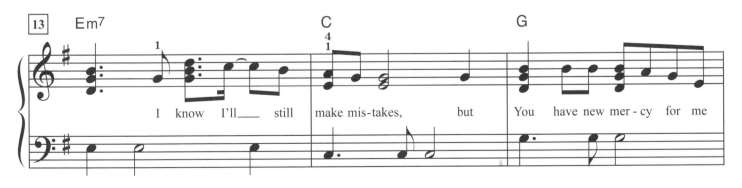

I know I'll____ still make mis-takes, but You have new mer-cy for me

Verse 2:
The wind is strong and the water's deep, but I'm not alone here in these open seas,
'Cause Your love never fails.
The chasm is far too wide; I never thought I'd reach the other side.
Your love never fails, oh no, oh no.
(To Chorus:)